Contents

Win Back Your Ex!

The Secrets to Rekindling Your Relationship

By C.K. Murray

Similar works by C.K. Murray:

Let Love Flourish: The Secret to Finding Your Kindred Heart

Body Language Explained: How to Master the Power of the Unconscious

A Reason to Smile: Finding Happiness in Life's Little Moments

Sex Science: 21 SIZZLING Secrets That Will Transform Your Bedroom into a Sauna

Sex Secrets: How to Conquer the Power of Sexual Attraction

Relationships can be hard.

But sometimes, the *hardest* part is getting them back. No matter how well you think a relationship is going, there will always be bumps and turns along the road. And when these obstacles become too much to manage, and the relationship too much to *salvage*, everything can come crumbling apart.

But what do we do?

What do we do if we want the relationship back? If we made a mistake? If our ex-girlfriend or ex-boyfriend, or ex-wife or ex-husband, is forever on our mind?

Nothing is perfect, and sometimes it takes a big change, a monumental change, for a person to realize what was missed. We all experience different stages of life in different ways. Although a couple may break up the first time around, there is always the possibility of a second-chance.

People can and do change. Sometimes all it takes is time. Time to mature. And time for the heart to mend.

Which is why nothing is out-of-reach. If you find yourself down and depressed, wishing you could win back your ex, don't give up! Don't let past mistakes prevent you from making it right, *once and for all*!

Remember: Love takes work.

So what are you going to do about it?

Understanding What Went Wrong

Relationships can go wrong for a variety of reasons. Some of us may have no idea until it's too late, till the relationship is already at death's door. In certain cases, a couple may completely split in one dramatic 'act' or argument. In rare instances, that argument is even violent.

Still, there are times when a split is nothing more than that: a separation of ways. Some couples may come to a decision amicably, deciding that they simply cannot go on and that it is best to part. However, even *these* occurrences leave something to be discovered.

Whether a tense break-up or a practical parting, the end of a relationship will inevitably change our lives. And for those of us who want another go, this can be the hardest thing in the world. But before we can win back our ex, before we can take another chance and make it finally work, we need to understand why it happened.

Before we know how to win, we must know why we lost.

The 7 Reasons Relationships Go South

The first step is honesty.

Not merely honesty with others, but more importantly, honesty with ourselves. Let's face it, most of us don't want to admit that we messed up. If a relationship ended on less-than-ideal terms (and almost *all* do), we're left wondering why. Many times, we put the blame on our ex. In some cases, we put the blame entirely on ourselves.

And this can be devastating.

What's important to remember is that relationships are never entirely one person's fault. They're always a two-way street. If a relationship slowly declined, it's because both parties involved did not find a way to mend the wound. Although one partner may be more responsible for the deterioration of a relationship than another, it is *both* partners' responsibilities to keep the thing healthy.

In thinking about where our relationship went wrong, we need to realize that there are many common causes. Sometimes relationships may even seem fine on the surface, when there is a deeper, undiscussed problem brewing.

Here are the top reasons that relationships end:

Lack of Shared Interests

Every relationship begins with interest. You're interested in getting to know your partner, you're interested in the potential for the two of you, and you're interested in the various things you both enjoy.

But sometimes theses interests fade.

As a relationship withers, the interests once shared also disappear. Did the two of you used to do a lot more things together? Did you used to watch movies together, go hiking together, go out to dinner, and read and relax and spend time simply enjoying each other's company?

By the end of the relationship, did it seem like the two of you no longer liked these same things? Was it as if the life had been sucked out of once enjoyable activities?

While it's good to share similar interests, it's important to remember that too many interests is also bad. If you and your partner are constantly doing *everything* together, things can get stale. Every relationship needs time for space, time for personal thought and fun with friends. If a relationship doesn't allow you and your partner to occasionally breathe free of one another, the relationship may not last.

Did the two of you lose sight of balance?

Emotional Downturn

We get into relationships for all kinds of reasons. A lot of the time, we may love somebody even if though we know all too well their faults. We'll even say that we love that special somebody *because* of his or her faults.

But what happens when faults turn to turmoil?

Emotional wellbeing is a critical part of any sustaining relationship. When we get to know our partner, we quickly realize that he or she is far from perfect. Although we can put shortcomings and failings aside, *embrace* them even, what happens when these issues grow too big?

Did our partner become obsessive, or overly insecure? Did he or she start to lose control of his or her emotions? Did the simple challenges of everyday life suddenly become too much to bear?

Was it drugs? Abuse? Did we love somebody, hoping that we could change that somebody? Did we recognize the pain and hurt in our partner's ways, and strive desperately to bring an end to that struggle?

Was our relationship destined to fail? Did one or both partners lose their wits? Did it become emotionality over rationality, leaving us confused and wanting? What role did self-destruction or mutual destruction play?

Were we ever emotionally compatible to begin with? Did we lack a firm understanding of emotional intelligence?

Differences in Character and Values

A main reason for emotional issues is a deficit in character. When we talk of character, we speak of honesty, integrity, honor, and hard work. We speak of responsibility and assertion. Character means that we strive to improve ourselves, to accelerate personal growth through positive means.

Of course, what's positive to one may not be positive to another.

When it comes to a lasting relationship, perceptions of 'character' hinge on values. We all have things that matter more than others. Some people want stability—a steady job, career, and living space—other people value freedom and flexibility, spontaneity and creativity.

When the values of partners do not closely align, it is difficult to keep the relationship alive. Shared values are the lifeblood of partnership. By embracing shared values, we allow love to grow organically. This is the key to romantic attachment.

If you valued exercise and clean living, but your partner valued relaxation and indulgence, over time these differences would cause separation. So think about why you entered the relationship... Did you believe you shared something with your special somebody?

By the end of the relationship, did you realize the truth—that your partner was not who you thought he or she was? Were your differences in value too large to overcome? Were the two of you incapable of changing values? Or, at the very least, tolerating new ones?

Inauthenticity

This is another major problem that leads to breakup. Many times we get into a relationship and we feel good. Over time, as things get tougher, we desperately try to hold onto that good feeling.

So what do we do?

Well, most of us end up 'forcing it.' We try to be something we're not, we try to be what we think our partner wants, and we try to force the fresh and fun times we once knew. 'Forcing it' is different than merely trying to make things work. 'Forcing it' is about putting so much effort, so much wasted energy, into disguising our troubles and creating something that *cannot* last.

Instead of focusing on changing the things causing our lack of enjoyment, we merely pretend that nothing is wrong.

When you pretend to be interested or value the same things as your partner, the relationship can falter. Over time, this lack of authenticity causes us to struggle. Although it's good to keep an open mind and share things with your loved one, it's important to never forsake your core values.

If you forsake your core values, you cease to be the person your partner liked in the first place. That is, assuming you weren't faking it from the very beginning...

No Conflict Resolution

Couples will struggle if there is no capacity for conflict resolution. If you and your partner were always bickering, constantly fighting and arguing and complaining, there was likely a bigger issue at play.

When couples are incapable of conflict resolution, they resort to emotionally damaging each other. It becomes a game of who was right and who was wrong; other considerations of compromise go out the window. Some couples try to sweep the problems under the rug in hopes that they won't resurface.

Couples that last will address their issues upfront in order to continue living harmoniously. Couples that fall apart will be unwilling.

Spirituality/Religion

Religion is a big part of many people's lives. There are numerous belief systems and lifestyle choices directly influenced by religious doctrine. Even if an individual isn't particularly religious, spirituality can certainly play a role. For many individuals, spirituality and religion offer guiding principles. These principles inform the way an individual may live his or her life.

This is not to say that individuals with differing religious perspectives can't live together. Heck, even atheists and devout religionists can live happily ever after. The important thing is not to necessarily *agree* with one perspective, but to *respect* it.

You may not agree with the tenets of a given sect of Christianity, but you at least respect that your partner does. You respect that your partner believes in something, and follows his or her faith for better living.

Even so, some people become so entrenched within a religion, that they cannot endure a relationship with somebody *outside* that religion. Certain partnerships may fall apart as fundamental religious differences leak into everyday aspects of life.

If your partner thinks you will go to Hell for doing something—but you don't think so and don't care—the relationship may crumble.

Lack of Communication

Communication is the cornerstone of a healthy, lasting relationship. When we communicate, truly communicate, we are speaking through more than mere words. Over 90% of communication is nonverbal, and couples often forget the power of body language.

If you aren't talking with your partner about the small things and the big things, then you aren't going to develop a lasting trust. Instead, you'll turn to other means for expressing or suppressing yourself. You may use friends, coworkers, or even cheat. You may also turn to drugs and alcohol to silence your unexpressed feelings.

When these means are used, the critical thread between partners is snipped. And it can be very hard, very difficult, to restore that line of communication.

Now that you understand some of the main reasons for why relationships fail, it is time to take a deeper look inward. Are you ready? Are you *truly* ready to change the things that didn't work before? Are you willing to sacrifice for a second-chance, or will you simply resort back to old and familiar ways?

The choice is yours...

Mending the Heart: The Best Way to React After a Breakup

Here's the good news: breakups are never set in stone.

Now here's the bad news: you have to be patient.

The first thing to do after having a breakup is to assess whether or not you even understand what happened. That's not to say you need to understand all the factors that led to the breakup—these will come with time. No, no, the important thing to remember *immediately* after a breakup is the terms of that breakup.

Every breakup has a set of rules. Sometimes these rules are unspoken, other times they are explicitly discussed. And it's upon you to recognize them.

Is this a full-fledged breakup or were the words "timeout" or "break" used in order to indicate a temporary distancing? Did the breakup occur after a big argument when the two of you were emotionally overheated?

Did you actually sit down and discuss that the relationship was over, or was there some wiggle room allowed?

When a couple discusses 'breaking up,' both parties understand that things were not going well. Although one partner may want to give it another go, both partners realize that the relationship has weakened.

Did the two of you agree that it was best to part ways? Did one partner essentially end it? Did a partner walk out, or move out, or cut you out from communication? Have you heard from your partner's friends that he or she no longer wants a relationship?

At times when a relationship has ended, both partners are not on the same page. One may be still trying to figure out if it's actually over, while the other has already started to move forward.

Occasionally, the relationship had withered so much that neither partner cares nor is surprised when it ends.

But what if you know that the relationship ended? What if you know that the two of you have officially 'broken up,' but still feel like there is another chance?

Are you still not ready to call your partner your "ex"?

Well then get ready. It's time to make sense of the confusion and the turmoil, and see the truth. It's time to know, once and for all, if your ex still wants you back. And this all begins with knowing the signs.

KEY Signs Your Ex Wants You Back!

Sexual attraction is more obvious than we're sometimes willing to admit.

The science of sexual attraction dictates that we look for certain clusters of behaviors and attitudes. If we don't know what to look for, we're screwed. We'll go through life never really knowing how others feel, and lacking the confidence to act.

So don't be clueless!

If you want to win back your ex, you need to be realistic. You need to look for signs. These signs may take a while to manifest, as breakups can be very hard on both partners initially.

Remember: be patient! If you want to win your ex back, you're not going to achieve this by suddenly and constantly bugging that individual. You aren't going to achieve this by immediately calling your ex and acting desperate. If anything, your ex will develop more negative emotions if you don't give him or her the space they need.

Before you make that first point of contact, allow yourself to sit back and recognize the signs that your ex is still thinking about you. Know that any one sign does not indicate an interest for certain. Instead, search for a *cluster* of signs.

Your ex may not always make these signs obvious, but instead will do so in many subtle ways. In today's highly connected world, the signs are everywhere.

Let's take a look. And remember, only *you* know your ex well. If you've seen certain behaviors before and know what they mean, keep an eye out for their reappearance.

Here are the signs:

Familiar Territory

In today's world, we have social networks such as Facebook, Twitter, and Instagram. All of these websites can be used to closely 'monitor' the behaviors and attitudes of an ex. Thus, it is no surprise that such networking tools may also be used to plan 'coincidental' encounters.

If you find yourself running into your ex at spots that the two of you used to frequent, be aware. If an old coffee house, or shopping mall, store, bike shop, area, or something of the like happens to turn up with your ex—you're in for an awakening.

More often than not, your ex knows you could be at one of these places. If your ex doesn't want to risk running into you, he or she will simply avoid these places. However, if your ex saw online that you were at one of these locations, it is very easy for him or her to then 'accidentally' run into you at that locale.

Little Reminders

If your ex truly wants to break off from you entirely, he or she is unlikely to give you reason to see him or her again. Although he or she may say, "I want to remain friends," we all know this rarely works as it is intended. Most breakups result in an awkward tension. The ex-partners generally want to move on with their lives—assuming their serious about moving on.

However, if you find that your ex has left little reminders at your place, in your car, or somewhere where you frequent, this is a good sign he or she wants an excuse to see you again. If the two of you shared a place, look for seemingly meaningless objects like shampoo, toothbrushes, combs, etc. If your ex left clothes—clothes that may or may not trigger special memories—then there's a good chance that your ex wants a reason to see you again.

If your ex left you with a little keepsake such as a letter, note, toy, accessory, or photo—there's even more reason to believe that he or she still thinks about you. And still wants to see you!

In many cases your ex may pretend that he or she simply forgot about the item in question. Even if this is true, it may signal that your ex is subconsciously fixated on you. Our subconscious sex minds are very powerful forces!

The Dating Issue

Some people will immediately jump into an old relationship when the most recent one ends. This could mean that your ex gets back together with his or her ex-ex! It can also mean that your ex quickly goes for a new guy or gal.

If you find out that your ex has quickly entered a new relationship, there is reason to be curious. Moreover, if your ex finds ways to show-off this new partner, especially on social networks or in person, he or she may be trying to get a rise out of you.

Most times when an individual jumps into another relationship quickly, it occurs out of insecurity. That individual may find single life too painful. He or she may crave the familiar feeling, and may try to project feelings for you onto his or her new partner.

Social Networks

Nowadays, practically everybody has a Facebook. Whether you think the website makes relationships more superficial or leads to deeper connections—that's up to you. What matters is this: a lot of people are on social media, and thus a lot of people will see what you share.

If your ex is suddenly flaunting his or her new partner, this could be a tactic to incite jealousy. Again, know your ex's style. If this seems like something he or she may do, it could very well indicate that he or she wants to show you what you're missing. On the other hand, sharing this status may simply indicate a genuine contentment with the new partner.

Don't draw any definitive conclusions from social media without seeing the other signs. Your ex may hide a new relationship from you as well. If he or she doesn't want to hurt you, or doesn't want you to know because it might hurt the chance of you two getting back together— consider your options.

And if your ex is flaunting a new status about being single and ready to mingle, analyze the situation. Is he or she actually the kind of person that will go buck wild? Have his or her friends communicated a desire to see you again? Is your ex merely pretending to be happy about single, when in reality he or she wishes for the security of a relationship?

If you find your ex liking or posting on your statuses, photos, and shares, this is a good indication that he or she wants to reopen the lines of communication. And while this alone does not mean he or she wants you back, it is certainly an opening for you to make a move!

Drunken Confessions

Some swear that alcohol is a truth serum. While science has yet to confirm this, we all know that alcohol can make us forgo rationality in favor of emotionality. If your ex sends you drunk texts or calls you when drunk, he or she is certainly thinking about you.

In fact, any kind of text or call, sober or drunk, is a good sign. Although trying to have a meaningful conversation with a drunk ex is probably not a good idea, it at least gives you an excuse to continue the convo the next day when that individual is sober.

Be wary. Drunken calls or texts may be an effort to get physical. If your ex is clearly not thinking clearly, you should put off the 'hook-up.' Negotiating the 'friends with benefits' territory can be very tricky, especially with somebody with whom you shared a meaningful past.

Understanding the various degrees of "hook-up" will make this much easier.

The Tone

Notice the tone of voice. The softness of voice. The way words are spoken. If you have a conversation with your ex, and he or she takes long pauses, speaks softly and slowly, this is an indication of attraction. By contrast, hurried, louder, and clipped speech indicates a disinterest in talking with you. This may be deliberate or unconscious.

When we still care for somebody, we truly listen to what they're saying. We often say less than if we aren't attracted (unless we're blabbering because we're nervous). Most times, however, we say less—and this is easily explained. Merely hearing the sound of our ex's voice is enough to please us.

Calls and Texts

If your ex calls for no real reason, or mentions something she or he forgot at your place, or asks for something random ("remember that auto-shop where you got that deal?"), then your ex is thinking about you.

If he or she calls or texts to wish you a happy birthday, he or she is giving you an opening.

Still Hanging Out

Being friends with your ex can be difficult. Few people are actually able to stay close friends with their ex's, especially if both partners are now in new relationships. In most cases, once the relationship has been over for a while, the ex, the ex's friends, and all other mutual acquaintances are more or less phased out.

But occasionally people can make it work. Still, this doesn't mean that the thought of getting back together isn't at the back of the exes' minds. Most men and women will stay in touch with their exes because this keeps the door open—or at least slightly cracked.

Think about it. Seldom do we keep friends and acquaintances in our lives unless we see a benefit in doing so. And what other primary benefit could one derive from somebody he or she *used* to enjoy romantically? Aside from the slim possibility, the glimmer of hope that, well…

Okay, so there are some of the key signs that your ex is thinking about you. Only you know your ex, so if you see that he or she is acting one way over another—it's up to you to know. Some girls or guys may try to make their ex jealous by jumping in a relationship. This may indicate that they actually care about their ex. Others may opt to stay single for a long time, indicating that they still want to keep the chances open for a rekindling.

But "rekindling" is easier said than done. If you want to make your ex come running back to you, you need to have your mind and your body right. You must make it a priority to get what you want when you want it.

Instead of sitting on your laurels, making the same mistakes as before, start being proactive!

Your ex may just be waiting for you…

What to do about it: Secrets to Rekindling Your Relationship

If you want to win your ex back, you need to start subtle. After a break-up, emotions are tender. Even if you were used to being very blatant and forthcoming with your ex, now is not the time to continue. Instead of spilling out your heart, or making it painfully obvious that you are "dying" to get back with your ex—try these steps in this order:

Starting Small

This means anything that is harmless. Remember, you don't want to further the damage. You want to slowly earn back your ex's trust and understanding. In today's world this means something as simple as 'liking' or commenting on a Facebook status, or sending a short text.

Many people think that by reigniting an old memory right away, they can win back their ex. More often than not, however, this is ineffective. Don't try to dredge up some old, cherished memory or express your innermost feelings.

Although it is possible to say something along the lines of "I still love you," this tactic is usually only effective in the romance flicks. Try to stay away from these emotional outpourings, again, for one simple fact: the post-breakup mindset is different than the pre-breakup mindset.

This should be commonsense to most people, but yet most people don't seem to carry through on this. Telling your ex that you need him or her, still think about him or her all the time, and can't live without him or her, will likely only cause confusion and more hurt. It will make your ex unsure as to your motives, and may lead him or her to trust you far less than ever imagined.

If you want to win back you ex, start with simple easy gestures and simple pieces of communication. Text before calling, and certainly connect on social networks before calling. Taking these informal steps allows you to test the waters.

For now, just stick to texting or communicating online. Calling will come later.

Still, be sure to reference something that he or she will know. While it is not wise to reference a special time between you just yet, by all means *do* reference a minor event or occurrence from your relationship. Or better yet, reference something you never got—a shirt, or pair of sneakers, or underwear, or trinket you 'forgot'.

For instance, come up with an excuse to text or post on social media.

If you text, you might say something like:

"hey! Do you remember the name of that restaurant your dad liked for happy hour?"

"omg did see what happened in walking dead?"

"what's up?? You don't still have my coffee maker do you? :)"

"I think I just saw your dog's clone…"

"It's waay too nice out to be at work ☹"

Don't readily express why you are texting. Allow the question or statement to elicit an organic response. No need to seem overly mysterious, but you don't need to totally enumerate your reasons either. Be concise and to the point, but add some flavor. Whether using an emoticon, an exclamation point, or some private lingo you guys once enjoyed, add a little something extra to your text.

The text should invite further communication. You want to work from something harmless and relatively meaningless, to something more important. Have a goal in mind. Obviously you want to win back your ex, but what's your short-term? Do you want to schedule a day and time where you and your friends, and your ex and her friends, can hang out? Remember, don't push the idea of meeting your ex one on one under date-like circumstances—not yet.

Text sparingly and never immediately reply. You want your ex to think that you have other things to do. You don't want to seem desperate or impulsive. Never reveal too much and don't reply readily to any advances your ex makes. Keep it light, like friends and nothing more. And then get into calling.

Making the Call

If your ex has been texting or even calling you up to this point, unprompted, you have a little leeway in making your first call. If, however, the only reason your ex has texted or called you is because you have texted or called first, you need to be a bit more careful.

However, some people prefer a call and are more likely to respond to those than to texts. When making the call, it is important to be mindful. What this means is that you are existing in the moment. You are dynamic and fluid, reacting to your ex's speech tone, volume, and regularity. Allow yourself to change your own tone, volume, and regularity. Do not worry about how you *expected* the phone conversation to go.

Embrace a state of mindful singularity.

Consider what you're doing when you call. Obviously phone calls are more intimate and the mere sound of your voice can unearth memories. Although you want to react dynamically to your ex's tone and voice, you also want to be sure to come in with a game plan. Why are you calling? What do you say to start off the conversation? Obviously, your ex might find the call intrusive, so it's up to you to start it off lightly and nonthreateningly.

Brief convos are the best. No more than a couple minutes. And be the one to end the conversation. Say something like, "Oh, sorry I gotta go, maybe we can catch up later though."

Communicate that you want to talk to your ex at some later point: "If you want, give me a call this weekend, I should be around." Be vague enough to elicit curiosity about where you'll be and what you'll be doing—but be certain to communicate that you *will* be open for future dialogue.

As always, be sure to maintain a happy and casual demeanor. You want your ex to think that you're okay being broken up, that the power is in your court and you don't need to flaunt it. Be sure not to make any direct references to what happened or how good the two of you used to have it.

If your ex wants to bring up these topics, do not cut her off. Instead, gently steer the conversation into lighter topics as tactfully as you can. And end it.

End it.

You need to be the one to end it—this cannot be said enough. It doesn't matter who ended the relationship or if it was mutual. What matters is that *you* end the phone conversations, always leaving something for your ex to want. Always ensuring that your ex didn't say everything he or she wanted to say; and didn't hear everything he or she wanted to hear.

Handling the Rebound

Of course, sometimes things don't go so easily. Your ex might be in a new relationship. Most times, this is a rebound to fill the void left in your wake. However, if the relationship lasts more than several months, your ex may be falling for this new partner.

In this case, there are several things you can do.

You can (a) incite jealousy by referencing other friends, guys, girls, and the like in your texts, phone calls, and social media statuses and photos. You can put on a happy, go-lucky face and show how much fun you're having without your ex. When you talk to your ex, you can mention casually the things you need or have to do. You can say things such as, "hey listen, I gotta go, we're all about to head out," or something like, "we'll have to catch up later, [girl and/or guy] and I are going to the movies." More or less, anything that signifies you may be hanging with somebody else—and enjoying it. At the very least, this will keep your ex guessing. At its most powerful, it will leave him or her overcome with jealousy.

However, if you find that making your ex feel jealous is *just not you*, you can elect for an alternative. Plant seeds in his or her mind concerning the nature of what you two used to be. Make him or her feel that you're doing well. If you don't want to incite jealousy, don't mention anything about what you're doing. In fact, talk little of yourself and casually ask your ex how things are on their end. If you know that he or she is currently dating somebody, make no mention of them.

While it may seem like the courteous thing to do is to ask your ex about his or her new partner—this is wrong! The last thing your ex wants is for you to say something along the lines of "I'm glad the two of you are happy." Remember, your ex wants a sign that you are still thinking about him or her. He or she is waiting for you to signal that you would fight for him or her, that you still care.

If your ex mentions his or her new partner, keep your tone as calm and casual as possible. Don't pass judgment and don't ask further about the relationship. Simply note that you heard what your ex said—"oh yeah?"—and allow him or her to continue along that line of dialogue if desired. But don't feed it.

After several phone conversations, texts, and/or social media interactions, it's time to take the big step. *Plunge*, more like.

At this point, you have but one goal. Meet up with your ex!

The Reuniting

You've gotten to the final step, but your work is far from over. This is where you really need to put your thinking cap on. Why did the two of you break up? If there were a variety of issues, what was the underlying problem—the main one? Are you going to show up to this meeting the same as before? Or are you going to make the change necessary to make this thing finally work?

When setting up the 'date' with your ex, be sure not to call it a date. Simply ask if he or she wants to meet up. Make it friendly and fun, such as at a coffee shop or a sporting event, or for lunch, or for a walk outside. For the first meet-up, it's best to choose a public place. Don't immediately opt for some private trip to the woods where it's just the two of you. Instead, go where there will be others. This is less threatening, and conveys that you are not trying to force the thing.

Give your ex a gentle but brief hug upon meeting, and be sure to continue the conversation in a 50/50 fashion. Don't hog the conversation, and certainly don't sit there silent like a gargoyle either. Express an interest in your ex's current happenings, and don't, *don't* go off talking about your romantic past together.

Show your ex how you've changed. You need to be positive and upbeat. If your ex thought you were a scrub before, dress nicer. Change your appearance if you have to. Show that you're not emotionally unstable anymore, or lost and confused, or obsessive and compulsive, or struggling to find yourself. Use your words and your body language to convey a new you. That is, a new, *authentic* you.

Have several of these 'dates,' keeping them casual, but progressively limiting the exposure to other people with each successive date. In other words, you are slowly making these meet-ups more intimate. You could start at a ballgame, work to a popular restaurant, work to a small café, work to a walk on a boardwalk—you get the idea.

Getting it Right

Judge the way your ex perceives your efforts. Is he or she becoming more loose around you? Has he or she mentioned your romantic past with increasing regularity? Do the two of you feel like things are going swimmingly?

In order to go from these low-key dates to opportunities for romance and physicality, you need to simply judge the situation. With each successive date, work in physical contact. Gradually progress from hugs and bumps and playful pushes or touches, to hand-holding and head-leaning. Judge your ex's reaction each time.

Bring the dates to a bar or club setting, then a dinner date—a private dinner date. If you reach the point of sex, it's up to the two of you to decide where to go from there. Are you thinking about getting back together? Do you want to be 'friends with benefits'?

Listen to your heart and your head. But never allow your heart to fully control you. Keep your head on your shoulders, and remind yourself why the relationship failed before. And never, *never*, slip back into those old, foolish ways.

Stay winning.

A Special Note:

Thank you for reading *"Win Back Your Ex! The Secrets to Rekindling Your Relationship."* If you enjoyed reading this book and would like to be included on an email list for when similar content is available, feel free:

http://eepurl.com/WWDVL

As always, thank you for reading.

And may you continue to live healthily and happily.

Sincerely,

C.K. Murray

Other works by C.K. Murray:

1. *Mindfulness Explained: The Mindful Solution to Stress, Depression, and Chronic Unhappiness*

2. *Emotional Intelligence Explained: How to Master Emotional Intelligence and Unlock Your True Ability*

Printed in Great Britain
by Amazon

25283943R10030